Ordinary Miracles

Ordinary Miracles

Inspired by
A COURSE in MIRACLES

Angela Dudley

BALBOA.
PRESS

A DIVISION OF HAY HOUSE

Balboa Press books may be ordered through booksellers or by contacting:

Balboa Press
A Division of Hay House
1663 Liberty Drive
Bloomington, IN 47403
www.balboapress.com
1-(877) 407-4847

ISBN: 978-1-4525-4029-0 (sc)
ISBN: 978-1-4525-4030-6 (hc)
ISBN: 978-1-4525-4028-3 (e)

Library of Congress Control Number: 2011917811

Printed in the United States of America

Balboa Press rev. date: 10/26/2011

Dedicated to
The Holy Spirit

Acknowledgment

I am forever grateful to my family. You are the special relationships the Holy Spirit uses to call me home: Christian, Amy, Abigail, Andrew, Audrey, Adam, Frank, Dick, Betsy, Katie, Cathy, Don, Denny. I want to love everyone as much as I love you.

I thank my ACIM study group for all you have shared with me, and all you have allowed me to share with you: PJ, Rian, Marion, Lou, Ben, Terry, Christine, Jo Ellen, Eleni, Arancha, Luba, Dan, Richard, Marsha, Joy, Jorge, Stewart, Pamela, Johanna, Warren. You are my life teachers; we are healed together.

From the Author

I sat in my car on a cloudy February day, waiting to meet up with a friend. As I wondered how to spend the next half hour, it suddenly occurred to me that I could probably find a book in the trunk of the car.

I often bought books, tucked them away in the trunk, and then forgot all about them. When I retrieved *A Course in Miracles* that day, I found it curious that I had no recollection of purchasing the book. Twice before, in 1983 and 1997, friends had encouraged me to read the *Course*. Both times I perused and then dismissed it. This time, I recognized the book that would change my life.

This is an example of the kind of "ordinary miracle" that happens every day in all our lives. We hardly notice them. To me the word ordinary means the regular or everyday condition of things, the way a thing exists in its basic and natural state. Here's a beautiful message from the *Course* in Chapter 1 of the Text:

> *Miracles occur naturally as expressions of love.*
> *The real miracle is the love that inspires them.*
> *In this sense everything that comes from love is*
> *a miracle.*

After studying the *Course* for about a year, I began receiving encouragement from the Voice Within to write down the loving thoughts I was receiving as I read. The Voice Within goes by many names. My favorite is Holy Spirit, a name I have

lovingly carried forward from my Catholic childhood. Whatever the name, the Voice Within resides in each of us, our Gift from God through which we remember the way home.

I am neither a scholar nor an accomplished poet, but I am the sister/brother of you, the reader. I may or may not be aware of our connection, but the Holy Spirit knows it. What I do know is that the love that surrounds and joins us is more profound than anything we have imagined. The joyful connection that we share is more real than these words on a page that I try to use to acknowledge our oneness.

The quotations in this book are from the public domain portions of *A Course in Miracles*, Combined Volume (Third Edition) 2007, published by the Foundation for Inner Peace, PO Box 598, Mill Valley, CA 94942, USA, www.acim.org.

I am deeply grateful to the Foundation for their continued publication of *A Course in Miracles*. It is but one form that the Holy Spirit uses to teach us what we really are and how to remove our blocks to love. It happens to be the form that reaches me.

The views expressed in this book are solely mine. Thank you for allowing me to share them with you. As the *Course* teaches, it is only by giving to each other that we will recognize all that is given us.

Angela Dudley

Contents

Prologue

This holy instant would I give to You.
Be You in charge. For I would follow You,
Certain that Your direction gives me peace.

from Lesson 361

Holy Spirit, as I wake today,
Give me every word I need to say,
Bless the pure intent of my request,
Lead me kindly to Your gentle rest.

Every choice that I will face today,
Every cloud that seems to block my way,
I will place them in Your loving hands,
Yours the task to always understand.

Everyone who knocks upon my door,
Every heart that seeks to be restored,
Beyond my little voice Your words will flow,
Perfect comfort only You would know.

Everywhere the Son of God is found,
In that place we stand on holy ground,
Past these worldly forms that I can see,
The stronger One Who always waits for me.

Holy Spirit, as I wake today,
Take the simple words I try to pray,
Take my love and all I yearn to be,
And give them to my Father now for me.

The Miracle
of Peace

Father, my home awaits my glad return. Your Arms are open and I hear Your Voice. What need have I to linger in a place of vain desires and of shattered dreams, when Heaven can so easily be mine?

from Lesson 226

How quietly the song of peace is sung,
What angels I have found myself among!
How gentle now the Voice within my mind,
In stillness, all the beauty I would find.

Every foot is set upon the road,
Spirit gently lifts each heavy load,
All of us are where we're meant to be.
Listen! God is calling you and me.

Not a single error I once saw,
Withstands the love of God's delightful law.
The unimportant dreams I thought I'd found,
So softly slip away without a sound.

My vision now is but the goal of peace,
From every judgment I am now released,
Bathed in stillness, held in holy light,
Spirit has restored my perfect sight.

The truth is that I am God's holy Son,
Already have my bliss and joy been won.
Nothing left for me to do or say,
I've been in Heaven for a while today.

Simply do this: Be still, and lay aside all thoughts of what you are and what God is; all concepts you have learned about the world; all images you hold about yourself. Empty your mind of everything it thinks is either true or false, or good or bad, of every thought it judges worthy, and all the ideas of which it is ashamed. Hold onto nothing. Do not bring with you one thought the past has taught, nor one belief you ever learned before from anything. Forget this world, forget this course, and come with wholly empty hands unto your God.

from Lesson 189

PEACE

Did you think you had to save the day?
Without your guidance God would lose the way?
Let it go.

Was sacrificing joy to be the cost?
Behold your sins, or else God's love is lost?
Let it go.

Did you believe that love could pass you by?
That happiness for you might be a lie?
Let it go.

And if you ever counted on a friend,
Would disappointment find you in the end?
Let it go.

Did you think your heart would prove unkind?
Your spirit much too small for God to find?
Let it go.

Did you imagine God was far away?
And couldn't hear the tearful words you pray?
Let it go.

Did you think the world was cruel and mean?
A place where peace refused to intervene?
Let it go.

Did you never think you might be wrong?
Must you always be the one who's strong?
Let it go.

Release control, your complicated plans,
And go to God with open, empty hands.
Let it go.

All little things are silent. Little sounds are soundless now. The little things of earth have disappeared. The universe consists of nothing but the Son of God, who calls upon his Father. And his Father's Voice gives answer in his Father's holy Name. In this eternal, still relationship, in which communication far transcends all words, and yet exceeds in depth and height whatever words could possibly convey, is peace eternal.

from Lesson 183

How lovely the sea that kisses my feet,
The spray that sparkles my face,
But what I adore as I stand at the shore,
Comes not from the form but the grace.

Majesty reigns in the height of the tree,
Centuries of shade 'neath the bough,
As I learn release I find Your peace,
In the gift of eternally now.

The arms of the child that circle my neck,
The laughter that sings in my ears,
The world rearranges with so many changes.
Yet love gently covers the years.

The warmth of the sun that taps on my glass,
The jasmine that sweetens my door,
The daffodil glistens, the river listens,
But Spirit beckons with more.

Surpassing the beauty around me,
The still, kind Voice in my heart,
Calms the storm, forgives the form,
And joins what was never apart.

How many sorrows will I accept,
And put myself to the test?
What tiny lives must I survive?
'Til I finally shift and say, "Yes."

Today we will not doubt His Love for us, nor question His protection and His care. No meaningless anxieties can come between our faith and our awareness of His Presence. We are one with Him today in recognition and remembrance. We feel Him in our hearts. Our minds contain His Thoughts; our eyes behold His loveliness in all we look upon. Today we see only the loving and the lovable.

from Lesson 124

I love you more than ecstasy,
You never leave My mind.
I've set your worth in vast expanse,
You *are*, neither cruel nor kind.
I raise you up with certain strength,
You are glory unconfined.

Feel the breath of air you take,
I'm closer than the air.
Look into another's eyes,
And you will find Me there.
I am the Voice inside your mind,
The peace for your despair,
And even when you turn from Me,
I answer every prayer.

Let go the sorrows binding you,
Awake in light today.
I lift the anger from your back,
Watch it drift away.
I give you still and gentle bliss,
Let Me lead the way.

I know the sins you think you own,
Hear Me, they are not true.
The cross was never yours to bear,
Take rest from all you do.
You are the breadth and depth of joy,
The world created new,
Every loveliness and grace,
Are all I see in you.

Salvation is a promise, made by God, that you would find your way to Him at last. It cannot but be kept. It guarantees that time will have an end, and all the thoughts that have been born in time will end as well. God's Word is given every mind which thinks that it has separate thoughts, and will replace these thoughts of conflict with the Thought of peace.

from the Workbook, Part II-2

I come to You with empty hands today,
Because I have not found a better way.
I do not come because I'm wise or smart,
But rather to release a weary heart.

My image of my brother makes no sense,
And so I come to You without defense.
Reveal the sacred brother I have missed,
Lift us in Your arms to utter bliss.

I languished while insisting I was right,
I turned my back on kind and loving sight.
I claimed the dark when truth was ever bright,
Within me, always waiting, was Your light.

The thought of peace is yet a choice for me,
When aggravation screams its sorry plea.
When sorrow and depression beg to stay,
God Himself provides another way.

No longer do I want the stressful dreams,
A world that truly isn't what it seems.
Within my mind God placed His holy feast,
I only need to give my thoughts to peace.

I live forever held within the light,
God's thought of peace remains my pure delight.
When joy alone expands my quiet mind,
Then only love is there for me to find.

"I rest in God." Completely undismayed, this thought will carry you through storms and strife, past misery and pain, past loss and death, and onward to the certainty of God. There is no suffering it cannot heal. There is no problem that it cannot solve. And no appearance but will turn to truth before the eyes of you who rest in God.

from Lesson 109

Every sorrow laid aside,
Not a single gift denied,
I rest in God.

I reached out, You were so still,
All I wanted was Your will,
I rest in God.

Unto You I've finally come,
All the chaos now undone,
I rest in God.

Every fear I gave a name,
Nothing left for me to blame,
I rest in God.

Angry outbursts You have soothed,
Each attack has been removed,
I rest in God.

Every one invited in,
Yet to be and might have been,
I rest in God.

I am comforted and safe,
Certainty replaces faith,
I rest in God.

Every burden that I bore,
Lifted now and ever more,
I rest in God.

All the sins I thought were mine,
Forgotten with the end of time,
I rest in God.

Grace is acceptance of the Love of God within a world of seeming hate and fear. By grace alone the hate and fear are gone, for grace presents a state so opposite to everything the world contains, that those whose minds are lighted by the gift of grace can not believe the world of fear is real.

from Lesson 169

Your promise that I'll see a different world,
The moment I remember I was wrong,
Makes me want to open up my heart,
To find the love outpouring from Your song.

Every irritation that I feel,
Covered by Your hands becomes a pearl.
Every tragedy I think I see,
Surrounded by Your grace transforms the world.

Every time my anger wants to speak,
Help me pause to listen for Your Voice.
When I cling to righteous self-defense,
Remind me I can make another choice.

Here I am, the Son You always love,
Lift me now into Your perfect peace,
Shine Your light inside my holy mind,
At last my every sorrow is released.

I take the journey with you. For I share your doubts and fears a little while, that you may come to me who recognize the road by which all fears and doubts are overcome. We walk together. I must understand uncertainty and pain, although I know they have no meaning. Yet a savior must remain with those he teaches, seeing what they see, but still retaining in his mind the way that led him out, and now will lead you out with him.

from the Workbook, Part I, Review V

You were there when I awoke today,
I'll not forget the words you had to say.
"I am your brother, come to lead you home,
Take my hand and do not feel alone."

I left my dream to wake and follow you,
The road I'd never seen and yet I knew.
You saw my fear and offered me your smile,
Peace and joy took hold with every mile.
I wasn't sure from when and where you came,
If we are brothers could we be the same?

You said you still recall the doubt I feel,
But now you know that it was never real.
You showed me how to listen and to pray,
And there it was, the old familiar way.
The Holy Host was gathered in a throng,
As we neared I heard their lovely song.

Together for a moment at the door,
Lifted to the light forever more.
Now and then a whisper that I'm missed,
All the saints are gathering in bliss.

The Miracle of Forgiveness

Only forgiveness can relieve the mind of thinking that the body is its home. Only forgiveness can restore the peace that God intended for His holy Son. Only forgiveness can persuade the Son to look again upon his holiness.

from Lesson 192

I would remember you,
When once upon eternity we lived,
And only God surrounded us in light.
Without the body's sickness or its pain,
Our holy rays extending ever bright.

I would forgive the world,
That taught me how to count in gain and loss,
And take from you to multiply my wealth.
Instead of separation in the dark,
Between us just the light of God Himself.

I would remember you,
The playful friend who only knows my joy,
The sweet companion of my holy peace.
No longer kept apart by space and time,
Open and connected and released.

I would forgive the world,
Dividing into shades of right and wrong,
Isolating hearts that would be one.
We're blissfully dissolving in the light,
To sigh at separation now undone.

All this forgiveness offers you, and more. It sparkles on your eyes as you awake, and gives you joy with which to meet the day. It soothes your forehead while you sleep, and rests upon your eyelids so you see no dreams of fear and evil, malice and attack. And when you wake again, it offers you another day of happiness and peace. All this forgiveness offers you, and more.

from Lesson 122

Forgiving is remembering
That you and I are free,
And all the scams the ego plans,
Insane conspiracy.

Forgiving is forgetting how
We made each other cry,
No more the song of who was wrong,
Nor words to justify.

Forgiving is the letting go
Of all we thought was right,
Let joy expand as Spirit's hand
Leads us into light.

Forgiving is the certainty
That only love is true,
What holy mind could be defined
By anything we do?

Forgiving is the giving up
The fearful world we made,
To find the peace of sweet release
For all who've been afraid.

Forgiving is an open heart,
Our comfort and our care,
The perfect bliss and happiness
That we forever share.

Vision has no cost to anyone . . . It can only bless.
from Lesson 27

❧ *FORGIVENESS* ❧

Above all else, I want to see,
A world in pure serenity,
Where friend and foe need only *be*,
Transformed by love's simplicity.

Above all else, I want to see,
Sacrificial lambs are free,
Blissful in our unity,
Spirit gently comforts me.

My Name, O Father, still is known to You. I have forgotten It, and do not know where I am going, who I am, or what it is I do. Remind me, Father, now, for I am weary of the world I see. Reveal what You would have me see instead.

from Lesson 224

I prayed today for healing of my friend,
That pain, at last, be brought to quiet end,
But still I see the sickness and the grief,
The anxious, restless days without relief.

Perhaps it is my sight that needs a cure,
For only Spirit's vision will endure.
The world I see is not outside myself,
I want to choose a source of truer health.

I need not see the Son of God in pain,
But rather hear as Spirit calls our Name.
I'm sorry I have seen a world like this,
My clinging to the past I now dismiss.

Forgive me, friend, that I have seen you weak,
Your glory far outspans the words I speak.
I set aside all guilt for my mistake,
The promises of sacrifice were fake.

I would not see you suffer one more day,
I would restore the truth that I betray.
You are a gift who's come to save my life,
My gratitude replaces every strife.

Holy Spirit, take my willing heart,
And adding all the strength that is Your part,
Bless and heal my vision of the earth,
That I might know its true and happy worth.

Connect me to the ones You've given me,
My judgment ends and thus I set them free.
Sweet innocence, enduring love, my friend,
In light and laughter ever we ascend.

Father, forgiveness is the light You chose to shine away all conflict and all doubt, and light the way for our return to You. No light but this can end our evil dream. No light but this can save the world. For this alone will never fail in anything, being Your gift to Your beloved Son.

from Lesson 333

I had a dream about you that wasn't true at all,
I thought you called me sinful, I thought you made me small.

My pain was so defeating, I felt so low and mean,
You said to me so softly, "But you only had a dream."

The more that I accused you, the more I made you sad,
You said to me so tearfully, "A dream was all you had."

We both were so unhappy, we decided then and there,
To hold each other blameless for a dream we didn't share.

What need of my forgiveness for a thing you didn't do,
I would not trade your beauty for a dream that isn't true.

My mind can still remember, we're never what we seem,
So I'll forgive myself for believing in the dream.

No matter how I see you, my perspective isn't real,
The only thing eternal is the love for you I feel.

When angry words are spoken that keep us far apart,
Error can't destroy the peace that's safe within my heart.

You are my perfect blessing, the holy bliss I've known,
We'll each forgive our dreaming; together we'll go home.

Forgiveness paints a picture of a world where suffering is over, loss becomes impossible and anger makes no sense. Attack is gone, and madness has an end. What suffering is now conceivable? What loss can be sustained? The world becomes a place of joy, abundance, charity and endless giving. It is now so like to Heaven that it quickly is transformed into the light that it reflects. And so the journey which the Son of God began has ended in the light from which he came.

from Lesson 249

I'll forgive you and you'll forgive me,
We'll both be as happy as summertime tea.

Everyone's in Heaven, no one went to hell,
We're all as playful as a recess bell.

I'll bless your joy, and you'll bless mine,
We'll dance beyond the end of time.

You're a child of the light; why, so am I,
Home-baked cookies and my favorite pie!

I can't hurt you and you can't hurt me,
And that, my friend, has made us free.

The way back home once seemed so far,
But we just forgot who we truly are.

You're the sparkle of summer, I'm the whisper of a song,
Like the wind is happy and the river is strong.

God is waiting with no demands,
He sees us coming, hand-in-hand.

Violets are red and roses are blue,
I forgive me and you forgive you.

Christ's vision changes darkness into light, for fear must disappear when love has come. Let me forgive Your holy world today, that I may look upon its holiness and understand it but reflects my own.

from Lesson 302

Were you there when they crucified my lord?
Have you found the light within that he restored?
Or that love's the only gift you can afford?

Teach them love, for that is all that we can be,
When they've irritated every ounce of me,
Touch the place where Spirit's light is all I see.

Once I thought he meant for me to bear his cross,
That finding God was done through sacrifice and loss,
If I trust my inner Voice, beware the cost.

Be not afraid, he knows the cross was an extreme,
He bids us not repeat the sacrificial dream,
Our little love is all it takes to be redeemed.

All the world has ever learned was of his pain,
Learn again he isn't hurt by our disdain.
"Forgive them, Father," was his simple, sweet refrain.

Learn from joy, for that is only what we are,
The grace of God within our hearts is never far,
No fearful dream could ever leave the faintest scar.

Were you there when they crucified my lord?
Know his heart and yours are ever in accord;
Gentle bliss will always be our true reward.

God's world is happy. Those who look on it can only add their joy to it, and bless it as a cause of further joy in them. We wept because we did not understand. But we have learned the world we saw was false, and we will look upon God's world today.

from Lesson 301

FORGIVENESS

We wept because we did not understand,
We pouted when life did not go as planned.
We argued when a friend did not agree,
We bound ourselves, then cried we were not free.

We felt attacked which justified our hate,
Believing mercy often came too late.
We sought control and put ourselves in charge,
Surprised, when chaos grew so very large.

We blamed each other for a world awry,
Assumed forgiveness was not worth a try.
We looked about and thought we saw the truth,
Relied on silly egos for our proof.

We did not know the universe itself
Could never multiply our inner wealth.
We did not see how much we had to give,
The utter peace in which we're meant to live.

We did not choose the easy, blissful path,
We made mistakes and then forgot to laugh.
We thought we were alone, adrift, apart,
But God Himself still held us in His Heart.

How patiently the Holy Spirit smiles,
Transforming our recriminating files.
With all our condemnations laid aside,
Heaven's door so gently opens wide.

How quietly we find ourselves within,
Releasing every tear that might have been,
Recalling that we never left to roam,
God is here and we are ever home.

The Miracle
of Joy

I am not the victim of the world I see . . . you are making a declaration of independence in the name of your own freedom. And in your freedom lies the freedom of the world.

from Lesson 31

❧ *JOY* ❧

Entitled to salvation from the world I've made,
I'm living in the light, and I'm not afraid.
There are no debts that must be paid,
No terrible laws to be obeyed.

No sacrifice required, no miracle refused,
No sin of which I've been accused.
Detached with joy and a bit bemused,
Nothing to gain and nothing to lose,
It was just a dream that had me confused,
I'm neither abuser nor the abused.

I'm totally loved and totally free,
And all I've created is saved for me.
I choose to be happy, I choose to see,
And to dance in God for eternity.

We do not ask for what we do not have. We merely ask for what belongs to us, that we may recognize it as our own. Today we practice on the happy note of certainty that has been born of truth.
from Lesson 107

No matter what I do today,
Despite what I might choose to say,
God's grace still belongs to me.

When I remember to observe,
Which teacher I have picked to serve,
God's light still belongs to me.

When kindness cannot get a start,
Frustration reigns within my heart,
God's peace still belongs to me.

Although I think I'm at my worst,
My ego, quick to answer first,
God's love still belongs to me.

When all I see are my mistakes,
A thousand years before I wake,
God's bliss still belongs to me.

What disappointment I might feel,
Can never make my judgments real,
God's truth still belongs to me.

Whatever lack I think I see,
I am as God created me,
God's joy still belongs to me.

We thank You, Father, for Your guarantee of only happy outcomes in the end. Help us not interfere, and so delay the happy endings You have promised us for every problem that we can perceive; for every trial we think we still must meet.

from Lesson 292

❧ *JOY* ❧

My guilt is all in my head,
As I cling to all that I dread,
Tickle me, Jesus, so I can laugh,
I want to be joyful instead.
My fear has never been real,
Though I made it a very big deal,
Tickle me, Jesus, so I will know,
To be happy is surely to heal.
I have tried to live in the past,
Where the length of sorrow is vast,
Tickle me, Jesus, so I will see,
That only the love will last.

Tickle me, Jesus, in spite of my tears,
Tickle me, Jesus, in spite of my years,
Whatever my journey, whatever my path,
Just help me remember to laugh.

I've been angry about many things,
Every pauper who should have been king,
Tickle me, Jesus, so I'll be glad,
For all of the grace that you bring.
I've been certain that others were wrong,
Thought I'd sold my soul for a song,
Tickle me, Jesus, so I will know,
That Heaven is where I belong.
How I've kicked myself in the rear,
For every false idol held dear,
Tickle me, Jesus, so I will see,
The truth is simple and clear.

Tickle me, Jesus, in spite of my tears,
Tickle me, Jesus, in spite of my years,
Whatever my journey, whatever my path,
Just help me remember to laugh.

You will see because it is the Will of God. It is His strength, not your own, that gives you power. And it is His gift, rather than your own, that offers vision to you.

from Lesson 42

When I see you through my ego
I can only know I'm wrong,
Hear the anger in my brother,
And I'll surely miss his song.
I am the holy Son of God,
There's nothing I can lose,
Whenever I'm unhappy,
There's another way to choose.

I see the wispy fields of grain
That gently meet the breeze,
The trees that circle round me now
Are only here to please.
How quietly my thoughts are stilled
As Spirit brings His gift,
And all the cares of all the world
Are softly set adrift.

Although I still perceive the dream,
The corners of my mind
Are hinting at the memory
That's here for me to find.
Spirit sends a picture
Of a soft and lovely light,
My eyes are closed to welcome
God's joyful, perfect sight.

Salvation requires the acceptance of but one thought;—you are as God created you, not what you made of yourself. Whatever evil you may think you did, you are as God created you. Whatever mistakes you made, the truth about you is unchanged. Creation is eternal and unalterable. Your sinlessness is guaranteed by God. You are and will forever be exactly as you were created. Light and joy and peace abide in you because God put them there.

from Lesson 93

If I would know I am the Son of God,
What joyless day could ever come to me?
What gift my brother asks would I refuse,
Knowing that I own eternity?

If I would know there is a light in me,
Beyond all greatness I imagine here,
What kindness would I ever fail to give,
My worth surpassing all that I hold dear?

If I would know I am the home of joy,
No day would pass me by without delight,
No sadness that I've shared by mere mistake,
Would ever take away my happy sight.

If I would know that peace is where I live,
In soft serenity and ever still,
You'd take my hand and we would always be,
Safe and sure and cradled in God's will.

Blessed Spirit, I would know the truth,
Teach me all the wonders I forgot,
I hold, within, the vastness of Your love,
Laying down at last what I am not.

I am as God created me. Let us declare this truth as often as we can. This is the Word of God that sets you free. This is the key that opens up the gate of Heaven, and that lets you enter in the peace of God and His eternity.

from Lesson 110

 JOY

I am as God created me,
Tranquil, holy, graceful, free,
The bliss that will forever be,
The truth of my eternity.

The joyful Thought of God I am,
The peaceful dove, the gentle lamb,
The blessed Son, the perfect plan,
The light that shines in every man.

The dreamer now forgets the dream,
Each brother held in sweet esteem,
The mighty sea, the quiet stream,
All, in me, are now redeemed.

No touch of sorrow can I see,
No judge to give a harsh decree,
Simple, lovely harmony,
I am as God created me.

Not one thing in this world is true. It does not matter what the form in which it may appear. It witnesses but to your own illusions of yourself. Let us not be deceived today. We are the Sons of God. There is no fear in us, for we are each a part of Love Itself.

from Lesson 240

 JOY

My answer to you is always, "Yes."
You needn't be worried, you needn't guess.
Imagine your joy, your peace, and your bliss,
When you finally let go and remember this.

Enjoy the day, eternally now,
Don't trouble yourself with the why and the how.
The plan is Mine, as it's always been,
Take off your coat of guilt and sin.

Play in the happy dreams I send,
My grace is yours, it does not end.
The world of sorrow is not true,
I can handle it all much better than you.

You don't have to struggle to always be right,
Sit back, relax, and enjoy the light.
Come to Me and your troubles will cease,
I give you My laughter, My love, and My peace.

We walk to God. Pause and reflect on this. Could any way be holier, or more deserving of your effort, of your love and of your full intent? What way could give you more than everything, or offer less and still content the holy Son of God? We walk to God. The truth that walks before us now is one with Him, and leads us to where He has always been. What way but this could be a path that you would choose instead?

from Lesson 155

❧ *JOY* ❧

What joy to think we walk the path to God,
So holy are the steps we chose to trod.
We look around the world that we observe,
There's nothing here the Son of God must serve.

Spirit came when we released the lead,
Letting go of all we thought we'd need.
We set our feet upon the blessed way,
The light of truth will beckon, come what may.

All our loving thoughts are gathered here,
Saved for us, dispelling every fear.
What miracle that we have found this path,
Where all our errors leave no aftermath.

We walk to God, how wondrous our task,
Simple truth, no questions left to ask.
We walk to God, an awesome, holy thing,
Our open hearts are all we're asked to bring.

The Miracle of Truth

You have one test, as sure as God, by which to recognize if what you learned is true. If you are wholly free of fear of any kind, and if all those who meet or even think of you share in your perfect peace, then you can be sure that you have learned God's lesson, and not your own.

from the Text 14-XI, 5

When every day your joy begins at dawn,
When all your words compose a happy song,
When every fear you've ever felt is gone,
You've found the truth of God where you belong.

When all your kindness only can increase,
When all the lies the ego told have ceased,
When every worried frown has been released,
You've found the truth of God that gives you peace.

When understanding is not sought alone,
When you've relinquished everything you've known,
When only love and gentleness are shown,
You've found the truth of God that is your own.

When nothing done alone can ever please,
When Spirit's power does it all with ease,
When wholly loved is all you want to be,
You've found the truth of God in all you see.

Give Him the words, and He will do the rest. He will enable you to understand your special function. He will open up the way to happiness, and peace and trust will be His gifts; His answer to your words. He will respond with all His faith and joy and certainty that what you say is true.

from Lesson 98

Confusion is illusion; peace is the truth;
Joy, not facts, will be your proof.

God is always found within,
When you forget to name the sin.

Your brother cannot cause you pain,
Yours the choice to lose or gain.

Heaven's door is open wide,
It's up to you to step inside.

I could see peace instead of this . . . Peace of mind is clearly an internal matter. It must begin with your own thoughts, and then extend outward. It is from your peace of mind that a peaceful perception of the world arises.

from Lesson 34

I took the gifts You gave me and judged them by myself,
I chose my own perception and thought it was my wealth.

I looked around me daily and everything I saw,
Was touched with my opinion as if I were the law.

The burden was so heavy, I longed to lay it down,
If judgment were my function, then how could joy be found?

And then I finally heard You inviting me to rest,
Let go my condemnations, my choice of more and less.

How fearfully I've judged what I didn't understand,
I couldn't find my way, I didn't see Your plan.

"Let go these tasks you've chosen," Spirit said to me,
"Let Me be your vision and truth is what you'll see.

You praise and blame illusion; let go and come to Me,
Release all your confusion, My love will set you free."

If I would find a value in a world I have condemned,
The love received and given is the only faithful friend.

It isn't the tree that is lovely, but rather my joy in the tree,
All that is real in the world patiently waits within me.

Heaven is the decision I must make. I make it now, and will not change my mind, because it is the only thing I want.

from Lesson 138

So many times the ego wants to say:
"To do it right, it must be done my way."
But I want to choose Heaven instead.
The little things that please me for awhile,
Tomorrow they will all be out of style,
And I want to choose wisdom instead.

How I preach of all that isn't fair,
Forgetting that the strength of God is there,
I want to choose peace instead.
A friend departs and I'm intent to grieve,
Unaware of all I'll yet receive,
I want to choose love instead.

Another person messes up my plan,
I cling to all the anger that I can,
I want to choose kindness instead.
Something's always getting in the way,
It's hard to dance when feet are made of clay,
I want to choose joy instead.

I criticize the world outside of me,
Refusing what the Holy Spirit sees,
I want to choose vision instead.
I go to meet my brother in the dark,
And there I fail to see his lovely spark,
I want to choose light instead.

I try to make you guilty for my pain,
Denying that our union is our gain,
I want to choose oneness instead.
I fill the empty minutes of the day,
Unaware the sadness of delay,
I want to choose Heaven instead.

Heaven itself is reached with empty hands and open minds, which come with nothing to find everything and claim it as their own. We will attempt to reach this state today, with self-deception laid aside, and with an honest willingness to value but the truly valuable and the real.

from Lesson 133

Great Spirit, You have listened to my call,
Though ever my perspective is too small.
Of all the worldly goods that I have won,
An emptiness has never been undone.
I've treasured all the beauty of the earth,
But cried with each event that changed its worth.

The innocence of animals held dear,
Their loss an ever-present, silent fear.

Companionship of family and friends,
Sweet bodies moving surely to their end.

The temporary smile of pretty things,
Rust and tarnish waiting in the wings.

Hoping all my judgments would be right,
Anxiety still lurking in the night.

So many years of wandering afar,
Yet here inside was always where You are.

How perfect is the lesson that You teach,
Heaven's always been within my reach.
Every painful thought I now release,
In quite stillness our eternal peace.
No longer will I value what has none,
With open hands and heart today I come.

What if you recognized this world is an hallucination? What if you really understood you made it up? What if you realized that those who seem to walk about in it, to sin and die, attack and murder and destroy themselves, are wholly unreal? Could you have faith in what you see, if you accepted this? And would you see it?

from the Text, 20-VIII, 7

What if I knew the world wasn't real,
Full of pretend that was scripted by me?
What would determine the coarse and the cruel,
And what of the beauty, the earth, and the sea?

What would I think if it all didn't matter,
The wise and the foolish truly the same?
Whom would I love and whom would I bless,
With no one to credit and no one to shame?

What if I knew the world was a dream,
And I could let go and gently observe?
Each of us loving and asking for love,
And never a fearful god to be served.

What would I see if I knew what I'd done,
Erecting the chaos and laying the blame?
Would it be gone in a moment of truth,
Revealing the kindness that whispers my name?

How lovely the Voice that is singing within,
That treasures the purpose of heaven and earth,
And tells me my Father knows not what I do,
But only my light and my limitless worth.

And as you let yourself be healed, you see all those around you, or who cross your mind, or whom you touch or those who seem to have no contact with you, healed along with you. Perhaps you will not recognize them all, nor realize how great your offering to all the world, when you let healing come to you. But you are never healed alone. And legions upon legions will receive the gift that you receive when you are healed.

from Lesson 137

My journey home continues, and as I call for peace,
Your calming Voice within offers my release.

I listen to You now, You tell me I am healed,
I can change my mind; there's no shame to be concealed.

I tell You of the pain, both done and done to me,
You wait as I recount the crimes You do not see.

You kindly take my hands, and opening each fist,
You loosen every fear that never did exist.

The clamor of the years has come to silence now,
You wipe away the tears for every broken vow.

You ask me why I choose to cling to my distress,
Holding dear the sins I think I must confess.

While God forever knows I am His sweetest song,
Would sorrow be my choice, insisting God is wrong?

Tranquility is real while I hold You in my mind,
But often I get lost and think You're hard to find.

And yet it is my mind, and all the love I feel,
Remains, in all the world, the only place that's real.

You are before me now as I look upon a friend,
I'm lifted to Your light by everyone You send.

The healing that You give, I then will give away,
From my hands it leaves, so it can truly stay.

And legions of the world, whom I have never known,
Walk beside me now; I am not healed alone.

Today the legion of the future years of waiting for salvation disappears before the timelessness of what you learn. Let us give thanks today that we are spared a future like the past. Today we leave the past behind us, nevermore to be remembered. And we raise our eyes upon a different present, where a future dawns unlike the past in every attribute.

from Lesson 127

If I didn't believe in the past I could be in Heaven today.
I'd have no need for the pain that frightens my peace away.

Encounters would each be holy, now and innocent and new,
Every breath an adventure, an eternal point of view.

No history would ever tell me to protect myself from you,
I would see our ancient alliance, the only thing that's true.

I would see the light within you and also within me,
No grievances would linger to bind what must be free.

My joyful heart would open to see you as you are,
No injuries between us, reminders left to scar.

With ease I would surrender to Spirit as my guide,
And every sad exchange would be gently laid aside.

How gladly I'd be lifted, knowing I was wrong,
Trading my perspective for Heaven's lovely song.

I've come upon the gateway, in front of me at last,
I could be in Heaven today if I didn't believe in the past.

The Miracle
of Oneness

You will first dream of peace, and then awaken to it. Your first exchange of what you made for what you want is the exchange of nightmares for the happy dreams of love. In these lie your true perceptions, for the Holy Spirit corrects the world of dreams, where all perception is. Knowledge needs no correction. Yet the dreams of love lead unto knowledge. In them you see nothing fearful, and because of this they are the welcome that you offer knowledge. Love waits on welcome, not on time . . .

from Text 13-VII, 9

~ *ONENESS* ~

There is a place where you and I are one,
Our choice for joy is what can take us there.
A place where every fault can be undone,
Where kindness is the lesson we would share.

There is a place where you and I can laugh,
Our choice for peace is what will lift the gate.
A place where only beauty lays the path,
Our choice for love transforms the choice for hate.

There is a place where you and I can be,
The Holy Spirit sees what we do not.
A place of truth and sweet tranquility,
Our choice for grace inspires every thought.

There is a place where you and I can go,
At last we will desire only this:
That God, who's all we ever choose to know,
Is lifting us forever into bliss.

My sinless brother is my guide to peace. My sinful brother is my guide to pain. And which I choose to see I will behold . . . I can . . . see my brother sinless, as Your holy Son. And with this choice I see my sinlessness, my everlasting Comforter and Friend beside me, and my way secure and clear.

from Lesson 351

How long these separate lives we guard so well?
The snubs and wounds and slights we live to tell.
I see you standing there but I am here,
Your view is surely dark if mine be clear.
Encased in bodies, there we hide our fears,
Afraid of who will shun our many tears.

Separation hides our holy mind,
Until we sadly see both cruel and kind.
Duality proclaims what we are not,
The only Son of God has been forgot.
Our differences abound, we mark them well,
The limitless contained in tiny cells.

I hear the thoughts you prize and I'm appalled,
I've lost your lovely smile, your happy call.
And yet today I have a fleeting thought,
Of joy we shared when hurt and pain were naught.
Safe in God, together, you and I,
Happy unity that never died.

Our oneness still begets a blissful peace,
The spark that shines in each awaits release.
The garden in our hearts remains serene,
Although we chose to leave and live the dream.

The spark of light must surely wait within,
Sometimes I see it just inside your grin,
And then a hidden memory's undone,
We're lifted to the light, forever one.

What you are seeing now conceals from you the sight of one who can forgive you all your sins; whose sacred hands can take away the nails which pierce your own, and lift the crown of thorns which you have placed upon your bleeding head. Ask this of him, that he may set you free:

Give me your blessing, holy Son of God.
I would behold you with the eyes of Christ,
and see my perfect sinlessness in you.

And He will answer Whom you called upon.
For He will hear the Voice for God in you,
and answer in your own. Behold him now,
whom you have seen as merely flesh and
bone, and recognize that Christ has come to you.

from Lesson 161

⋘ *ONENESS* ⋙

In sleep I dreamed of gentle company,
Together we were lovely, happy, free.
The space between us there I could not see,
Which tenderness was other, which was me?

The power of that oneness in the night,
Sweet mystery I brought into the light.
Holy Spirit, teach me one more time,
Of all the love I had forgot was mine.

Was the one in sleep a friend I've known?
Who's the blessed one whom I was shown?

Spirit said my view is often blind,
The holy Son of God I cannot find.
And if I passed this one along the street,
I would not smile, nor recognize, nor greet.

It broke my heart to see what might be lost,
Belief in sin demands a bitter cost.
Lead me, Spirit, teach me how to see,
Each one who hears the Voice for God in me.

It is impossible that anyone be healed alone. In sickness must he be apart and separate. But healing is his own decision to be one again, and to accept his Self with all Its parts intact and unassailed.

from Lesson 137

My sickness must become the wall between,
The place where peace and joy cannot be seen,
Where you can't understand the pain I feel,
And so I prove our separation's real.

The sorrow and the emptiness I know,
In spite of the concern that you might show,
Will keep me in a place apart from you,
Where we will think our separateness is true.

In sickness I have chosen to retreat,
Afraid our union signifies defeat,
Afraid that if I offer you embrace,
Then all I think I am will be displaced.

The Holy Spirit sets a different road,
By choosing to lay down this heavy load,
Together is the only way I'm healed,
Sweet miracle I've foolishly concealed.

When all the laws of health the world proclaimed,
And all its facts have finally been named,
The world cannot explain what love can do,
The healing peace connecting me and you.

No one remains in hell, for no one can abandon his Creator, nor affect His perfect, timeless and unchanging Love. You will find heaven. Everything but this will fall away. Yet not because it has been taken from you. It will go because you do not want it. You will reach the goal you really want as certainly as God created you in sinlessness.

from Lesson 131

❧ *ONENESS* ❧

With separation sorrow has a voice,
Where darkness seems to be a valid choice.

We always fail to fix what isn't real,
Meanwhile Heaven's joy remains concealed.

As every broken child extends a hand,
Love's the only way to understand.

Kindness will be all that's asked of me,
Oneness is the gift that sets us free.

The problems of this world we cannot solve,
But given to the light they are dissolved.

How full of grace to know that we were wrong,
The Earth will sing when we compose the song.

A home in God is always what we share,
No limit to the love that's waiting there.

God does not forgive because He has never condemned. And there must be condemnation before forgiveness is necessary . . . Yet although God does not forgive, His Love is nevertheless the basis of forgiveness. Fear condemns and love forgives. Forgiveness thus undoes what fear has produced, returning the mind to the awareness of God. For this reason, forgiveness can truly be called salvation. It is the means by which illusions disappear.

from Lesson 46

We gathered in a worldly place, our plan was to escape,
Our complicated subterfuge was slowly taking shape.
So when the proclamation came that Peace was surely dead,
We looked into each other's eyes to find them full of dread.

Who would kill the precious Peace, we all had loved her so?
It wasn't me, so maybe you, and fear began to grow.
An inquisition was arranged to clearly place the guilt,
As each awaited questioning our alibis were built.

The first to come for scrutiny were Pleasure next to Pain,
Certain that the other one was deeply cursed with blame.
As Handsome strode into the room to smugly stand by Plain,
No matter all their differences they both were hiding shame.

Scarcity and Plenty came, Funny walked with Sad,
But all their accusations paled when Good came in with Bad.
Private thoughts laid bare that day, sins for all to see,
If you're the one who murdered Peace, at least it wasn't me.

Then as amazing as the first, the second herald came,
Peace was found, she wasn't hurt, her innocence remained.
Although our gladness filled us all, much was left to mend,
We all had tried to save ourselves as others were condemned.

When fear had taken over me, I never stopped to find,
That both of us were searching for the way to peace of mind.
So when I saw the light in you, and you the light in me,
Forgiveness brought our glad return to loving unity.

Sometimes we seek the darker place wherein we tried to live,
But Spirit sends reminders then of what we have to give.
We smile and nod to all in turn, we treasure every sight,
Within each one we now can see the ever-present light.

All that I give is given to myself. The Help I need to learn that this is true is with me now. And I will trust in Him.

from Lesson 126

 ONENESS

The Son of God is free to save himself,
The gift I give my brothers is my wealth,
With my loving thoughts the truth expands,
The way to peace was always in my hands.

Kindness only leads to ecstasy,
Laughter blesses our equality,
Lean on me and I will give you rest,
Love Itself will be our holy guest.

Nothing that is asked I cannot give,
Spirit is the strength with which I live,
How softly I am taught the way to see,
All I give to you is given me.

You who perceive yourself as weak and frail, with futile hopes and devastated dreams, born but to die, to weep and suffer pain, hear this: All power is given unto you in earth and Heaven. There is nothing that you cannot do.

from Lesson 191

I stood before the ancient redwood tree,
In my mind it gently spoke to me:

It is to you my branches surely nod,
You have made me thus, oh Son of God.
I am a form your kindness has become,
How quietly all madness is undone.
We reach for light, a place above to see,
A softer world where every prisoner's free.
The certainty that fills this lofty spot,
Tells of love you often have forgot.
In this peace that knows not death nor birth,
Miracles profoundly bless the earth.

I hear the Voice that God has sent to me,
The thought of light, my true identity.

Forgive the pain and all the tears I weep,
Love's sweet embrace is all I need to keep.

All of us are holy, all are one,
There's nothing God denies His holy Son.

The Miracle
of Innocence

You are not the victim of the world you see because you invented it. You can give it up as easily as you made it up.

from Lesson 32

You are the guiltless child of God,
His treasure and His joy,
You only dreamed eternal love
Could ever be destroyed.

You made a place of good and bad,
And then you called it home,
Abandoning your holy truth,
You thought you were alone.

God's Holy Spirit holds you still,
Gentle, safe, and true,
His Voice is here within your heart,
Whispering to you.

Spirit am I, a holy Son of God, free of all limits, safe and healed and whole, free to forgive, and free to save the world.

from Lesson 97

I don't think this body
Could be the strength of me.
"Yes," the Voice serenely speaks,
"You are spirit, you are holy, you are free."

Ever as my heart expands,
Letting go of my demands,
Then within my open hands:
The safety of the world.
How do hands so weak and worn,
Tired now from sorrows borne,
Hold the rose without the thorn,
And transform a broken world?

If these hands I now can see
Were totality for me,
How to reach across the sea,
To soothe a grieving world?
Though the call for love seems distant,
And my body so resistant,
Yet there comes the Holy Instant,
And the world is truly one.

Every thought still plays a part,
All the love within each heart,
A little willingness to start,
Unveils the lovely world.
All the burdens of the Son
Are now given to the One
Who magnifies our little sum,
To carry home the world.

You are a dream, oh body,
And not the truth of me,
"Yes," the Voice serenely speaks,
"You are spirit, you are holy, you are free."

The eyes of Christ look on a world forgiven. In His sight are all its sins forgiven, for He sees no sin in anything He looks upon. Now let His true perception come to me, that I may waken from the dream of sin and look within upon my sinlessness, which You have kept completely undefiled upon the altar to Your holy Son, the Self with which I would identify.

from Lesson 313

I set out on a walk one day with several stops to make,
I went with joy and a loving heart, peaceful, certain, awake.
First I came to a daffodil and stopped to see her dance,
Her yellow face and hint of spring—at once I was entranced.
Next I saw a lovely fawn, bespeckled and beautifully made,
There in the grass on the side of a hill, playful and unafraid.

I came to where a prison was built, and there behind its wall,
A prisoner with a hardened heart, the spark of life so small.
A large volcano down the road, rumbling, threatening, bold,
Daring the earth to hold its wrath, much darkness to unfold.
A garden gate appeared to me, inviting and so I knocked,
No answer came that I could hear; alas the gate was locked.

For many years I recalled that day, remembering all I'd seen,
A flower, a deer, the pain and fear; what could it really mean.
Then I asked the Voice within the truth of all that day,
With confidence I listened for what Spirit's Voice would say.

"No matter the pretty, the nice, and the sweet
to balance the coarse and the mean,
No matter how vast, or mighty, or loud,
beloved, it's only a dream."

I took that walk again today and all I saw was this:
The love that was sought and the love that was shared,
the peace, the joy, the bliss.
I came again to the garden gate where long ago I'd been,
With open hands and a happy heart, I easily entered in.

His patience has no limits. He will wait until you hear His gentle Voice within you, calling you to let Him go in peace, along with you, to where He is at home and you with Him.

When you are still an instant, when the world recedes from you, when valueless ideas cease to have value in your restless mind, then will you hear His Voice.

from Lesson 182

❧ *INNOCENCE* ☙

Forever have I been the stranger here,
Fearful that perhaps I walk alone,
Until the stillness once again returns,
And I recall an ancient song of home.

How long have I forgotten where the road,
That takes me to the peace I sorely miss,
The turmoil of the world but tells me true,
The song within my heart is not of this.

I'm haunted by the sound I must have heard,
A melody that takes my breath away,
How I yearn to hear it once again,
It lingers in the shadows of today.

Deep within my mind there comes a child,
Who softly sings my song of innocence,
A melody of purity endowed,
Removing any need for my defense.

The Son of God has ever called to me,
I cannot comprehend the bond we share,
How patiently He waits for me to sing,
The song of home that finally takes us there.

Sweet melody that waits within my mind,
To tell of innocence I cannot lose,
The song of God has never left my heart,
And evermore is always mine to choose.

In stillness we will hear God's Voice today without intrusion of our petty thoughts, without our personal desires, and without all judgment of His holy Word. We will not judge ourselves today, for what we are can not be judged. We stand apart from all the judgments which the world has laid upon the Son of God. It knows him not. Today we will not listen to the world, but wait in silence for the Word of God.

from Lesson 125

Nothing else is real,
But the quiet Voice inside,
Speaking ever gently,
Safe, in Me, abide.

All else disappears,
But that single, quiet nod,
Confirming in the night,
You know the way to God.

The quiet stillness comes,
The Voice within is true,
Whispering my name,
I always am with you.

I am lifted into peace,
Through no effort of my own,
The Voice is all I know,
Wake up, you are home.

Recalling what is real,
Spirit's Voice is always kind,
The flow of certainty,
You are ever in God's Mind.

I live within the Light,
The gift I can't destroy,
The wonder as I hear,
Behold, you are My joy.

I am in the likeness of my Creator. I cannot suffer, I cannot experience loss and I cannot die. I am not a body. I would recognize my reality today. I will worship no idols, nor raise my own self-concept to replace my Self. I am in the likeness of my Creator. Love created me like itself.

from Lesson 84

. . . and Jesus said . . .

How patiently I've waited for this day,
You're listening, at last, to what I say.
I am the way, the truth, and, yes, the life,
You never must again endure the strife.
We are the sons of love, the sons of light,
I have removed the clouds, restored your sight.

You've never been alone, I am with you,
I never leave because of what you do.
The anger and the errors are not real,
In spite of all the pain you think you feel.
Let go your thoughts and enter through your heart,
Heaven's real, you've never been apart.

Love has made you like unto Itself,
Together we're Its joy, Its truth, Its wealth.
Look beyond the grievances you've made,
To find no reason left to be afraid.
Take my hand, we're here at Heaven's gate,
You're just in time, and love is never late.

Under all the senseless thoughts and mad ideas with which you have cluttered up your mind are the thoughts that you thought with God in the beginning. They are there in your mind now, completely unchanged. They will always be in your mind, exactly as they always were. Everything you have thought since then will change, but the Foundation on which it rests is wholly changeless.

from Lesson 45

I thought that deep inside was mostly sin,
Helplessly I thought I couldn't win,
But You touched me.

So many days my ego got the best,
So tight my grasp of every fault confessed,
But You held me.

Projecting all the anger was my plan,
Wash the blood I thought had stained my hand,
And You heard me.

Philosophies remained an empty prize,
Worldly wisdom but a weak disguise,
And You knew me.

All I had to do was let it be,
The price of Heaven, after all, is free,
For You love me.

Have faith in only this one thing, and it will be sufficient: God wills you be in Heaven, and nothing can keep you from it, or it from you. Your wildest misperceptions, your weird imaginings, your blackest nightmares all mean nothing. They will not prevail against the peace God wills for you.

from the Text, 13-XI, 7

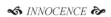 *INNOCENCE*

The Light of God beholds
You are Its brightest gem.
God does not forgive,
For God does not condemn.

Whatever you have done,
No matter what the strife,
Happiness remains
The purpose of your life.

Innocent little child,
Whom God does not deny,
You know not what you are
If fear can make you cry.

Think of only joy,
Every moment's new,
Hell does not exist,
Heaven's within you.

Love remains the truth,
Regardless what you see.
God is in your heart,
In tranquil certainty.

Epilogue

Into Christ's Presence will we enter now, serenely unaware of everything except His shining face and perfect Love. The vision of His face will stay with you, but there will be an instant which transcends all vision, even this, the holiest. This you will never teach, for you attained it not through learning. Yet the vision speaks of your remembrance of what you knew that instant, and will surely know again.

from Lesson 157

How do we speak of what cannot be said,
What never was written and never was read?
A love so much greater than we ever thought,
More than we hoped for, more than we sought.
The moment we knew, beyond hope, beyond doubt,
No one forgotten, no one left out.
Life without limit—gentle, serene,
No more a need to forgive or redeem.
Nothing to choose when the gift is so pure,
Freedom is born when we're perfectly sure.

The moment has passed but the thought will remain,
Nothing will ever again be the same.
Only a memory—the touch and the song,
But God ever lifts us to where we belong.